Discover Halloween

by Juliana O'Neill

© 2017 by Juliana O'Neill
Hardcover ISBN: 978-1-5324-3722-9
Paperwork ISBN: 978-1-53240-217-3
eISBN: 978-1-53240-218-0
Images licensed from Fotolia.com
First Edition
Published in the United States by
Xist Publishing
www.xistpublishing.com

xist Publishing

2

I like Halloween.

Halloween is in the fall.

5

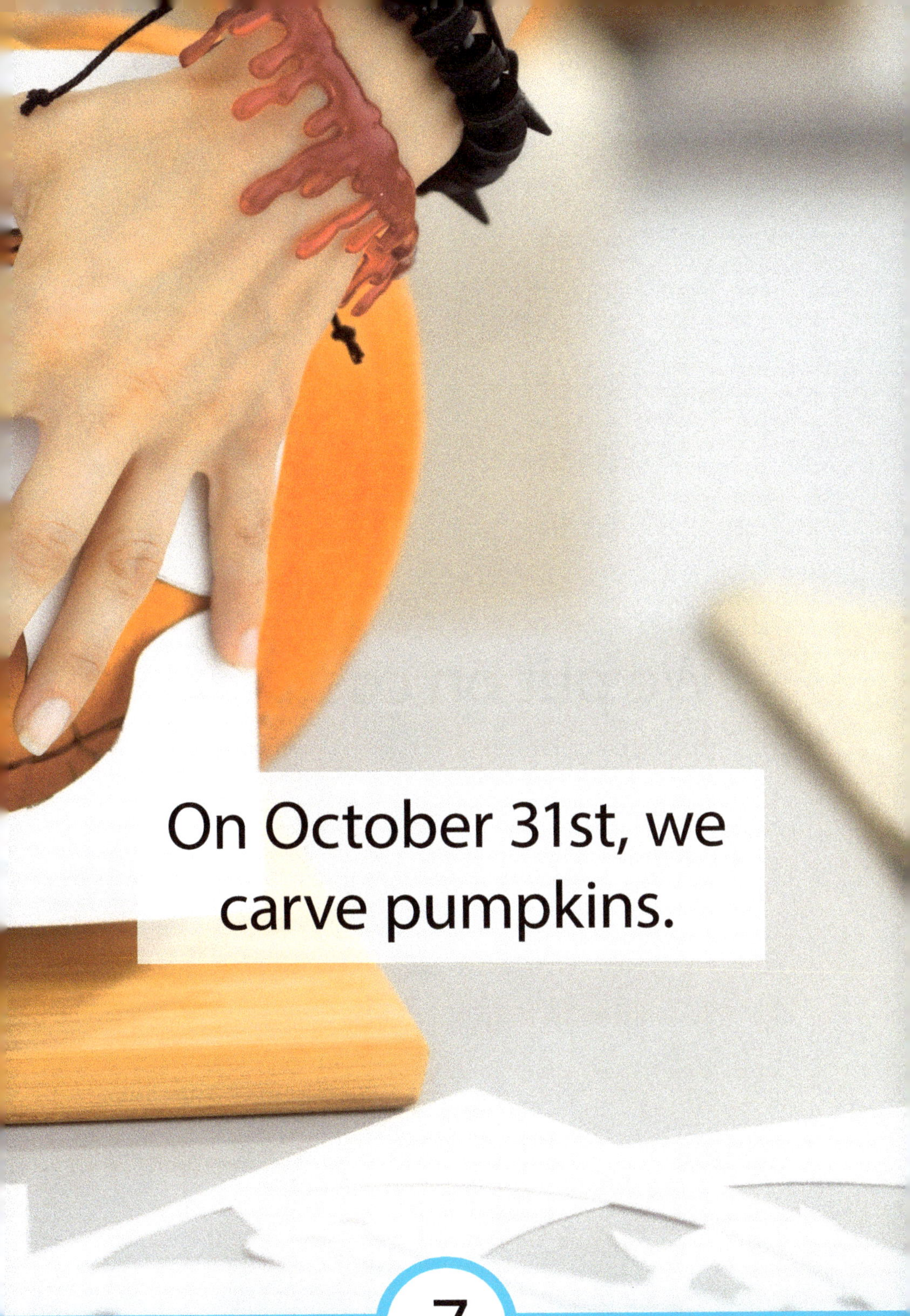

On October 31st, we carve pumpkins.

We put on costumes.

We grab our flashlights and go out the front door.

11

We go from house to house and see our friends.

At the door, we say, "trick or treat."

14

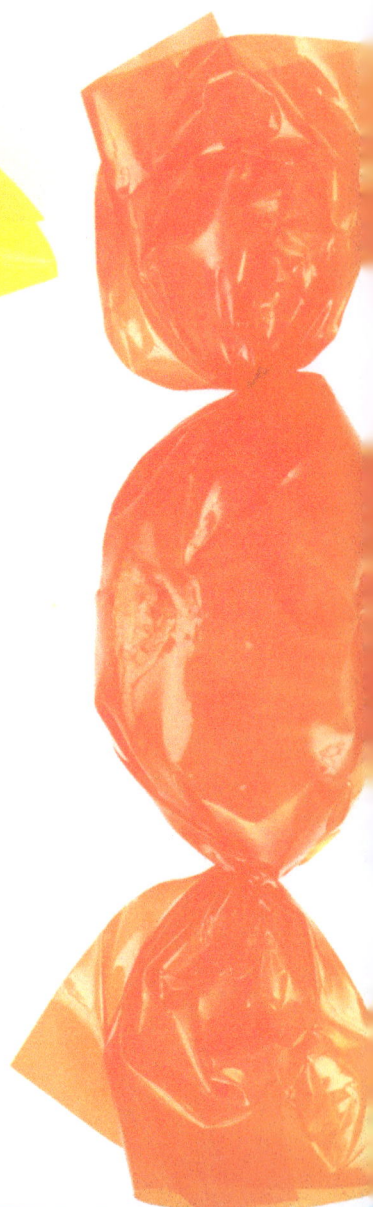

I got my favorite candy.
Thank you!

18

Some people wear scary costumes.

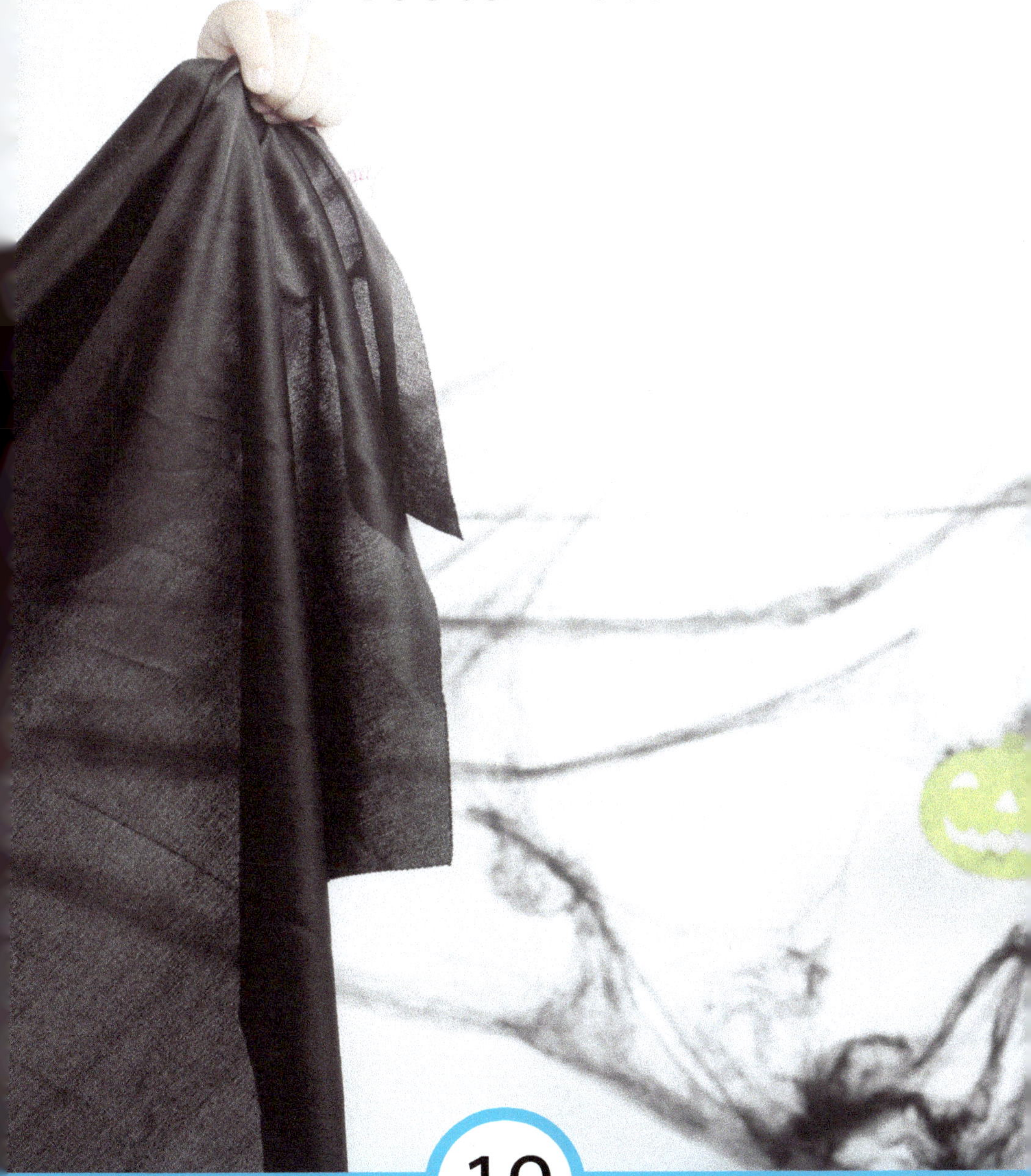

Some houses wear scary decorations.

I am not scared.

I know it is fun to pretend.

23

Halloween is a good night to celebrate.

25

At home, we sort our candy.

Then, we brush our teeth and say good night.

www.ingramcontent.com/pod-product-compliance
Lightning Source LLC
Chambersburg PA
CBHW052129150426
42813CB00077B/2671